Threnody

Threnody

poems by Donna Hilbert

MOON
TIDE PRESS

~ 2022 ~

Threnody

Editor-in-chief
Eric Morago

Editor Emeritus
Michael Miller

Marketing Specialist
Ellen Webre

Proofreader
Jim Hoggatt

Front cover art and interior art
Donna Hilbert

Author photo
Alexis Rhone Fancher

Book design
Michael Wada

Moon Tide logo design
Abraham Gomez

Threnody
is published by Moon Tide Press

Moon Tide Press
6709 Washington Ave. #9297
Whittier, CA 90608
www.moontidepress.com

FIRST EDITION

Printed in the United States of America

ISBN # 978-1-7350378-8-2

for my beloved family,
for Nathaniel
for my workshop
for Jill Young who has read every word since the first word
for Torey Eden, forever

Contents

VI

Foreword

"Say desire, which is the boat," writes Donna Hilbert in her newest collection of spare and poignant poems, *Threnody*...a lament, a wailing. Loss figures prominently in these poems, the devastating loss of her beloveds: her husband, tiny kittens, the felled trees where familiar herons had raised their young, dead seabirds lying on the sand, her mother—but what carries the poet forward is the thirst for beauty and presence. Desire keeps the poet and her reader floating over the abyss of despair...desire for full awareness, the longing to appreciate all of life, including everything from the hummingbird to the powerline. Coming through personal loss and then a pandemic, the poet gently shows the reader how to carry on, "In a fit of hope I wash and press white shirts..." and reminds us of the simple rituals like making risotto, "stirring until everything is tender," and listening to Beethoven. "I have had my fill of things that shine" the poet writes, inviting us into a deeper way of being. Rinsed of the superficial, Hilbert confronts what it means to be truly alive, knowing everything she loves is ephemeral. Daily she feeds crows, walks the beach, and claims: "Even a bird blind/might be a kind/of altar."

—Heather Swan, author of *A Kinship with Ash*

Man's life is error where, then is relief?
In shedding tears or wrestling down my grief.

    — *Laments* by Jan Kochanowski
    tr. Stanislaw Baranczak and Seamus Heaney

 In the dark times
Will there also be singing?
Yes, there will also be singing.
About the dark times.

    — Bertolt Brecht

We are your oracles—your Ammon, Delphi, Dodona,
and your Apollo

    — Aristophanes, *Birds*

I

Culling

I've seen them at work,
know what herons do,
how far they travel
in one flap of blue.

Walk in Winter

My dog and I stop to watch
as one by one, Heron brings
twigs washed up on shore
to spindly palms that line
the beach-side streets.

It's early winter, but Heron
doesn't seem to know, or mind,
that rain and wind will follow
bringing weather far less kind.

To what will come,
my sweet old dog is also blind.
O, for the peace of dogs who know
nothing of winter and letting go.

Pandemus

Upon a current flowing west,
a wide red swath divides the water.
I try to drown the thought of death,
but wish to know which curse is this
and what great beast is bleeding.

My ailing dog asleep all day,
my children grown and scattered,
sadness piles on sadness,
a layer cake of sorrow,
with icing made of daily dread,
and filling made of marrow.

Dirge

Here I am, standing under palm trees
listening to Great Blue Herons sing
a song like machinery grinding.

Yesterday, arborists sent by the city
knocked hatchlings to their death
in a frenzy of cutting and stashing
fronds, and birds, into dumpsters.

Did they know that herons mate
for the season, and return each spring
to the same trees to build their nests again?

In this spring of staying home,
I have watched the heron's industry,
carrying sticks from beach to tree
and back for more, building in tall palms.

The song in the tree is not the song in the sky.
Not every voice in the choir rejoices.

Instructions for Pie

Treat dough gently, love it
like the baby in your dreams.
Chose fruit of the season:
today peaches, tomorrow,
apples will be green.

And, always, there are lemons.
Come a sudden summer rain,
meringue falls like a hill of snow.
Don't despair!
The filling will still be delicious
with soft, tart, sweetness below.

Compression

I ease new socks from toe to calf to knee
to keep the threat of clotting blood at bay—
good for airplane travel in cramped space,
good for long days working on my feet.
I have to say, I like the way they hug
my legs and wish these socks could reach my hips
and grow beyond to case my body whole
with touch, the way I swaddled my sweet babes
in flannel for the calm of binding tight.
Who among us wouldn't crave a firm embrace
when flesh forgets the path to keep itself in place?

Tula

My dog believes she's seen a ghost,
when I return from travel,
assume a form again.

My first night back, she cries
outside the bedroom door
until I rise, command her day *begin*.

Jogger

I know him by his footfalls
The Angry Jogger—
pounding double-strike,
he claims the middle boardwalk,
won't yield to bike
or walker. I wonder what
he's running toward
or from. If he escapes
the chaser, will he know it?
If he gets to where he's headed,
will he recognize the door?

Walking the Palo Alto Marshes
in My Red Coat

Say mud flat, salt marsh, bittern, egret.
Say egret without thinking regret
one letter away.

Say morning is a gift.
Say the mud flat is a silver tray.
Say birds sing like an orchestra tuning.

I am looking for a prayer.
I am walking for the saving incantation.
I am working at metaphor.

Say blackbird.
Say red wings like epaulets of blood.
Say heart: red four-chambered room.

Say womb, breast, cradle, boat.
Say desire.
Say desire: dark and fathomless,

the iris of an eye, your eye, the sea.
Say desire,
which is the boat.

I am wearing my red coat against the cold.

Mallards Fly In

Soon they will nest.
Later, hatchlings will be stranded
trying to cross the street.
Not everything is solved by walking.

II

Grief

In the dishwasher,
nothing but spoons.

Blackwing

Which will go first
eraser or lead?
I ask, watching
my favorite pencil
turn in the sharpener.
Sliver of rubber,
barely a nub, answers:
write what you will,
what you won't
take back.

We Don't Believe in Rain

We don't believe in rain
in this beach city
where I sit in my parked car
not ready to go home.
Dog-walkers in flip-flops,
and joggers in T-shirts, go forth
as if the sun were shining,
as if the sun were always shining.

Dear Sadness,

You live in a saddlebag
cinched to my hip
by sinew and bone.
To walk with you is hard.
Please, forgive my complaint.

Others hurt more, I know.
When you were fixed
between atlas and axis
like a petrified necklace,
I hurt more.

It was hard then to hold up,
impossible to turn.

Bare

In gray of May, gloom of June
lush lavender jacaranda blooms.

By July, its glory strewn
it's just a tree of branch and leaf.

Exposed in blue relentless heat,
how naked now, I feel in grief.

Dear Husband,

You've been denied my extra portion,
killed as you were before the worst
thing happened. (I still won't say *die*
with its connotation of normal, order.)

This kill too fresh for ink to spill
its name, so let's just say that earth
quakes and oceans empty from my eyes,
eyes I thought would never fill again

with salt and water sufficient for such
sorrow, sufficient for such pain.

Hole

for T.E.

You looked good last night
in gold sweatshirt and jeans,
face alive with color,
as if you'd just walked home
from school in the cold.
The others were stunned,
so, I made a blanket of my body
to hold you, but again
you dropped into the hole
wide and dank as my world.

Since

for T.E.

Booze, cigarettes,
and, at last,
old age,
that rasp the throat.
Or, so I thought.
It's not.
Since your death,
every word
a gasp.

Sympathy Pears

Sympathy pears are paired
with apples and a promise
of shipping within two days.
Regular pears and apples
take longer to box and send.

Sympathy pears and apples
are suitable for painting,
but the artist must supply
the skull, the worm, or fly.

Sympathy pears and apples
arrive with no protocol of care:
simply eat or ignore, no chore
to water, prune, or keep abloom.

Dear Bereaved One,
eat, or not, while you ponder
a *Better Place, His Will,
Her Plan. Everlasting Love.*
Or none of the above.

Eclipse

Your death,
young one,
is the moon
blocking the sun,
but it does not pass,
is not undone.

III

Sight

One must look closely
to see the cardinal
in a maple tree.

Aimez-vous Brahms?

Tula, the poodle, rises to music,
walks the hallway to what calls,
lies down next to the sound: Brahms,
the only music that moves her.

First World Problem

Back porch crow
tries fitting two
Costco peanuts-in-the-shell
into a one-peanut beak,
caws for help.

Risotto

Down again. Tonight, it's the purple
of heirloom tomatoes,
I slice into olive oil, garlic, red-bell pepper,
short-grained rice, a pinch of saffron
or two. I add broth one ladle at a time.
I stir the rice and I am stirred
by Beethoven sonatas
alive in the fingers of Emil Gilels,
and stirred too by the winter setting that fills
the window I look through to the sea,
from my station at the stove.
When the Waldstein Sonata begins,
I cry into the copper-clad skillet
I use for sautéing petrale sole
and for making frittata and risotto.
No need for a special pan.
No need to steep a broth from scratch,
bouillon paste from a jar, plus water, will do.
Beethoven wrote thirty-two piano sonatas.
Emil Gilels recorded all but five
before he died unexpectedly in Moscow.
Sviatoslav Richter believed the KGB
had killed him, fearing he would defect to the West.
You might add lemon zest, capers, or olives,
if your risotto needs more zing.
All that really matters is the stirring
until every bit is tender, add broth, stir.

Auspices

While I watch for Crow,
a yellow-green hummingbird
shimmers himself
in late morning-light blue.
Message or messenger,
or something bright new?

Door

An open door is no small pleasure,
leading to a deck overlooking the alley.
Yes, there are powerlines,
but palm trees too, and birds perch
in either place without complaint.

Dammit

Here I am on the back deck,
watching a guy on a tall
extension ladder paint
my neighbor's house.
All week, I've nursed
a spark of indignation
that he and his co-workers
leave used face masks in the alley.

When they're gone,
I sweep the masks into a pile
and bank them at the edge of the house.
By morning, they've blown back to the alley.
I sweep again to make a statement.
The ritual continues: they drop masks,
I sweep, I swear, the wind blows.

But, this morning, I see him
climb the ladder. It looks unsteady.
I'm scared for him.
He must have felt my gaze,
for he turns a bit toward me,
a big happy smile on his face.
He says, *how are you?*
I say, *be careful.*
He says, *have a great day!*
I say, *you too.*
Now, dammit, we're friends.

Signs

Had a Piece Lately?
read the slogan on the pizza parlor's
sign in the town where I grew up.
This sent Mom & Aunt Lucy
into ripples of laughter I didn't understand
each time we stopped for lunch.

Mom & Lucy were The Toot Sisters
once for Halloween—
Prosti wore a red dress, Desti wore torn jeans.
Desti is poor, Prosti is rich,
Mom explained, twirling her sash.
I cut a doll from paper, named her Prosti,
crayoned her mouth a saucy gash.

Idea of Order in the Cupboard

The glasses must match like twin sisters.
The tall ones will stand in the back.
White fine bone cups from Great Britain
hang by their crooks from a rack.

Clean

Mother rinsed dishes in a mix
of hot water and bleach
and with the same noxious brew,
swabbed doorknobs and faucets.
Not even latches on gates escaped
her everyday war on disease.

That was before we knew
what plague lay in wait
to smite us and lock us in place.

Wherever you are, beyond the urn
in my closet, Mother, hear me concede:
you were right when you told me
a girl must be careful,
and *there's no such thing as too clean.*

For Mother, Whose Maiden Name Was German

From this porch swing
I look into the woods
beyond the highway,
and dream of you, Mother,

who didn't like the woods,
but loved a porch swing,
who liked horizons clean:
ocean beyond a bank
of sand, a backroad arrow
through billowing
seas of wheat.

You didn't like the woods,
but loved a porch swing.
O cradle of memory.
Your name, Zumwalt:
into the woods.

You didn't like the woods,
uneasy when the way
could not be seen.
How did you enter then
the pitch-black woods
unafraid, serene?

IV

Gratitude

For the brown pelican
diving into morning ocean,
I thank you, Rachel Carson.

In Terram Incidere

Now, dead birds on sand:
fifteen pelicans, cormorants
by the score, seagulls so numerous
we don't count them anymore.

Terns on their autumn trip
karr-reek past the browning sun.
Migrants, stay on the fly.
If you must fall,
please fall from a different sky.

Unreliable Narrator

Liberace was born in the Bronx,
the dream voice informs me,
but Wikipedia tells a different story
citing West Allis, Wisconsin
as the sparkly pianist's hometown.
This news shakes my faith
in the rest of the dream:
immortal poodle, talking newborn,
the Nebuchadnezzar connection.

2020

for Kari Gunter-Seymour

I sit on the back porch
crying into a book
about Appalachian women
cleaving to each other
in life and death.

It's hot for May. Still, palm trees stir
and in the neighbor's yard
friends play ping pong, passing time
in this season of seamless time.

Fear sits with me. I give him his due,
but don't know how to entertain him.
Then, from the deep unknown
my mother warns:

*Don't feed him, Donna June,
or he'll never pack up, go home.*

A Burning Somewhere

I snap a dazzling sunset photo
of the golden orb plummeting to the sea.
At first, I think my dirty window is the only filter:
panes glazed by offshore winds and coastal fog.

Then, I realize it's flames
in inland foothills, canyons, desert flatlands
that have rendered blue skies umber.
Slater, Lone Star, Creek, Bobcat, El Dorado,
to name a blazing few.

Death is the mother of beauty, the poet claims.
Does this hold true?
Always, a burning, always a fire.
Somewhere a hearth, somewhere a pyre.

* The italicized line is from "Sunday Morning," by Wallace Stevens

AQI 75

To walk onto a porch over-looking driveways, alleyways,
satellite dishes, X's and Y's of powerlines against a sky
newly blue after days and days of brown, gray, brown,
to sit under a red umbrella and listen to Charles Mingus
is a blessing, and one shade of blue will do.

A Blessing in August

I give thanks for the woman
wearing orange and pink,
walking the morning beach,
luscious against the water
startled blue with sunlight.

That Blue

that blue
entering fog
after the sun
up for hours
but hidden
that blue
where sky
and sea
form a seam
that blue
like milk
on a blue dish
barely seen

Lost

I have lost my wanderlust
having wandered,
having lusted.

Justice

In the down of leaf-dropping trees,

in the meadow, under flowers and weeds,
all seasons are ambient, all lesions benign,

no pigs go to market,
no pigs eat roast beef,
all bodies dine on seven

species of onion
in the down of leaf-dropping trees,
the wolf stays for supper,

grandmother pours wine,
soft camels sing
sweetly as troubadours,

inhaling inspiration,
there is no rumination,
in the meadow, under flowers and weeds,

sweat flows freely,
tears flow freely,
there is no word for shame,

prophets are well known
yet honored,
lost lovers return

with lost car keys,
prodigals return chastened
without celebration,

orchids grow wild
in the down of leaf-dropping trees,
Keats and Mozart grow old,

in this garden of composure,
Van Gogh paints
his child sleeping in a great lap of leaves

in the meadow under flowers and weeds.

Even

Even a bird blind
might be a kind
of altar.

Buried

A half-dozen kittens flat on the grass,
the first thing I saw from the car, one Sunday
when you drove me home from mass—
dead kittens arrayed across my dad's Dichondra.
I screamed, cried, *carried on.* I was seventeen.

You were twenty and soon returned to school
where you wrote daily notes on air-mail paper
about how it bothered you, my tears
for cats I barely knew. Something must be
wrong with me, you said, so much easy weeping.

I don't remember who wielded the shovel
that day, or when I stopped crying,
or where, exactly, everything was buried.

Apophenia

The morning after the slaughter
of hatchlings, a lone heron flies from the west
to a nest atop a palm tree. I walk the beach,
and in everything I see there is Heron:
in the carcass of a tree washed ashore
one root appearing like neck and beak
twisted toward the boardwalk
as if to watch for passersby.

Sometimes I think the eye is like the mind,
intent on meaning, in love with signs,
the way that after your death
I would see you, tall and lean
our dog on leash, distant walker
from land far, far from reach.

My Husband

Hated seagulls and hated salmon,
too much of both in Seattle,
when he studied at the "U."
Living in a dorm, you take the food
as given, and with it also take the view.

In my kitchen with its ocean view
salmon sizzles in a skillet,
it's sunset, and seagulls sweep
the dimming sky.

What would you think
of this place you left me, this meal
I make for another? A blessing not to see
what's coming, like the day two tons
of metal swept you from my sky.

Blue

My husband never liked the color blue,
though he loved the LA sky,
and lakes and seas and swimming pools.

When I wanted a dress, or car, or room
in cerulean or just plain blue, I told
him blue was green or gray.

Because our love was wide and deep,
he did believe in every word I'd say.

Seventh Game of the World Series and I Have a One-Day Breakdown

How 'bout them Dodgers:
your rhetorical change-up
from politics or personal
line-drive to the gut.

Why won't you say you love me?
Why don't you call your mother?
My questions, then your question
How 'bout them Dodgers.

We don't talk about the ways
our parents fouled us, or worse,
strikeout after strikeout of our own.
See the ball, hit the ball,

you taught our children.
Lesson enough? I wonder.
But, O those hot dog and peanut-
eating evenings, the cotton-candy

sky dissolving to deep blue,
us in the stadium with our crew,
spring, summer, sometimes fall,
See the ball, hit the ball

*How 'bout them Dodgers, think
they'll make it to the fall?* I'm told
that's what you were saying
when you biked into the sunrise

when the errant driver didn't *see*
you, didn't see that he would *hit*
you, end your season in the summer.
How 'bout them Dodgers.

From Sleep

Stupored from sleep, I survey my clothes.
Clothes left in the closet untouched
for a year, or longer, touch each garment
as if it were cashmere or silk,
hanging in a palace of goods
I could never afford, even dare enter.
Such is the breadth of my longing.

Turning to the task at my feet,
I rifle a basket of unfolded laundry
for my costume of sweatshirt and jeans.
Living from basket to hamper to basket,
I dress, lace my shoes, set out for a walk
to start one more day in the dark.

Flight

In my only dream of flying,
my sister who is sick is well.
She visits, dressed in bangles
shining like clean pennies—
the same color as her hair.
We burn with our own beauty;
we are sleeker than rooks.
We fly by private physics
through air, dry and thick as sand.
We rest on wire, above the city,
where people sing for our pleasure.
We know nothing of death.

Ache

What doesn't pinch, pouches
and looks suspicious.
What's the meaning of this patch
of peeling skin? The intermittent
stitch joining hip to belly,
what does *that* mean? My legs
awaken me at night with an ache so deep,
I struggle in vain to relax and sleep.

As a child, I screamed from the nightly clutch
of *growing pains* after days scaling trees,
then biking home to supper before dusk.
Now, I'm not young. Nothing grows.
My body is a house of cards about to shuffle,
a fallow land of falling dominoes.

dent de lion

Don't call me weed,
but love instead my golden
head dressing swards of green.

The sunshine of my flowering gone,
then love me in my second crown
of silver tuft and drifting thread.

River

Grief is a river, I tell my friend,
then realize what I say
makes little sense. She nods,
and I choke back my disclaimer.
Ill-fit metaphors slip from my mouth
when I'm at a loss in the face of loss.
And, I have faced loss enough
to know there's nothing right
or sufficient to say when death's maw
widens to swallow dear life away.

VI

On My Sunday Morning Walk,
I am Reminded of Wallace Stevens

Palm tree frond and heron wing are one,
or so it seems to me from where I stand.
Palm tree temple, heron priest,
and I, a congregant, alone.

February 2021

In a fit of hope, I wash and press white shirts
hidden in the hamper since last March.
I order lipstick, and a see-through make-up bag
with hooks to hang on any random perch.

Perspicere

I've come to love the power lines
crisscrossing the alley behind my house.

Birds pause here, between their quests
for food and water, to rest

until returning to nest in palm trees
across the alley, down the block,

across the street, and to places
that, no matter how I fix my gaze,

I can't quite know, I can't quite find.

Dear Laurie,

To identify the bird singing from the powerlines,
I pull *Birds of America* from its spot atop the bookshelf.
Remember, friend, when you gave this book to me?
Before your move to Texas? Or, was it after the returning
to California? Your grandmother's book
you said, she who also loved to name the birds.

How I grieved when you moved half-way across the country
with your family for your husband's better job.
I boarded the plane with your baby, barely three-months old,
while you wrangled the other children up the ramp.
It was December. Remember how we cried?

The new year began and with it, grief began in earnest.
Jobs soured. Friends divorced. In May, my father died.
When school was out, to staunch my tears,
Larry loaded our boys into the car
(which car? I don't remember)
and we crossed the desert states.
Craters, canyons, caverns, kitsch motels, the kids counted
dead critters on the highway all the way to Texas.

Hellish hot, the Texas summer, but Laurie,
you and I were glad to sit in misery together.
We passed the baby back and forth, refilled our icy drinks.
The children, keeping cool, wielded water guns and hoses.
The husbands talked sports, flipped burgers on the grill.
It was June.
Did we celebrate our birthdays, one day apart, together?

I don't remember the birds in Texas,
but mosquitos and chiggers
ruled the grass. Cicadas swarmed the backyard trees,
a visitation we'd not expected with its symphony of sizzle
and buzz as if a world were ending or beginning.
We could not have guessed which guests
would call upon us next. Some callers it's best not to expect.

Food

A banana, one day past green,
sliced into a bowl
with Cheerios and a spoon
of granola, then covered
with milk, is good
for breakfast and plain
enough to be communion.

Morning Again

Morning again, and I await
the crows who wait for me
to look away, that they might
snatch a nut or two
from the empty window frame,
where, at the same time
every day, I set a meal.
Legends say that crows
will leave a gift for those
who feed them, but after
months, all they leave behind
are empty shells and trails
of slime. Never mind.
All I want is a daily visit,
a bit of company on the porch.
In this the crows are faithful, kind.
I give thanks, and not reproach.
I've had my fill of things that shine.

Deer

Now that you have crossed the green,
I long to see your face again

turn to me as if to say good-bye.
You follow instead the others' lead

through maple, birch, pine, and weed.
I wish you rest in a grass-made bed.

Many Bottoms in the Basket of Despair

There are many bottoms in the basket of despair
as many as sparrows dropping (no end in sight)
from the wide and deep blue air.

And who among us even dare
to notice what lies sleeping right
beneath us in the basket of despair?

Remember the old dog, her shedding hair,
the endless sweeping, (day and night)
as if cleaning also cleared the air.

I've traveled backroads leading God knows where
without a roadmap, compass, or beam of light.
There are many blind spots in the carriage of despair.

Once, on a riverbank I thought I'd lost you, aware
of what might swipe you from my watchful sight,
I feared you swallowed by the wide and deep blue air.

I'm marking time now, trying just to bear
nightmare days and sleepless nights
lying with the boarders in the casket of despair
uncountable as dust motes in the wide and deep blue air.

Rosemary

You are the rosemary I add to the soup:
how you pressed pungent bristles
between thumb and finger,
how you lay sprigs atop red potatoes
glistening in olive oil, salt,
house alive with the fragrance
of vegetables roasting
on any given day of the week.

1,095 days past your death, young one,
I sometimes escape the earthquake
of absence upon awakening,
but daily remembrance, I never escape:
today, it was rosemary, yesterday,
blue sea glass washed up at my feet.

Lines Ending with Rumi

Heron feeding nestlings
in the Red Bud tree
brings me to my knees.
There are many ways to kneel
and kiss the ground.

About the Author

Donna Hilbert was born in Grandfield, Oklahoma near the Oklahoma-Texas border, but has spent most of her life in Southern California. She is a graduate of California State University, Long Beach, with a B.A. in Political Science, and from Phillips Graduate Institute, with an M.A. in Marriage and Family Therapy. Her books include *Gravity: New & Selected Poems*, Tebot Bach, 2018; *The Congress of Luminous Bodies*, Aortic Books, 2013; *The Green Season*, World Parade Books, 2009, *Traveler in Paradise: New and Selected Poems*, PEARL Editions, 2004; *Transforming Matter*, PEARL Editions, 2000; *Feathers and Dust, Deep Red*, and *Mansions*, all from Event Horizon Press. In 1994, she won the Staple First Edition writing award resulting in the publication in England of the short story collection, *Women who Make Money and the Men Who Love Them.* Her *Greatest Hits* chapbook, which includes her most anthologized poems from 1989-2000, was published by Pudding House. Her work is the subject of the short film *Grief Becomes Me*, by director Christine Fugate, which was shown as a work-in-progress at the Kentucky Women Writers Conference and is included in *Grief Becomes Me: A Love Story*, the documentary about her life and work. She writes and teaches private workshops in Long Beach, California, where she makes her home.

Acknowledgements

I thank Jerod Santek and the staff and board of Write On Door County for the generous residencies during which many of the poems in *Threnody* were written. I also thank the gracious editors of the following journals where poems in *Threnody*, occasionally in slightly different form, have appeared.

Chiron Review: Dear Husband, Eclipse, River, Since

First Literary Review East: Aimez-vous Brahms? AQI75, First World Problem, Unreliable Narrator

Gatherings an art & poetry project: Dirge

Golden Streetcar: Buried

Gyroscope: Risotto

Mansions: Culling, Justice, Walking the Palo Alto Marshes in My Red Coat

Nerve Cowboy: Compression, Lost, Signs

One Art: Dear Laurie, *dent de lion*, February 2021, For Mother Whose Maiden Name Is German, Grief, *Perspicere*, Mallards Fly In, On My Sunday Morning Walk I Think of Wallace Stevens, Rosemary

Red Shift: A Burning Somewhere, Clean

San Pedro River Review: Jogger

Sheila Na Gig: 2020, Ache, *Apophenia*, Dear Sadness, Hole, Many Bottoms in the Basket of Despair, Morning Again, My Husband, Walk in Winter, We Don't Believe in Rain

Shrew: Seventh Game of the World Series and I Have a One-Day Breakdown

Verse-Virtual: Compression, Food, *In Terram Incidere*, Justice, Seventh Game of the World Series and I have a One-Day Breakdown, Walking the Palo Alto Marshes in My Red Coat, A Burning Somewhere

Also Available from Moon Tide Press

A Burning Lake of Paper Suns, Ellen Webre (2021)
Instructions for an Animal Body, Kelly Gray (2021)
Head *V* Heart: New & Selected Poems, Rob Sturma (2021)
Sh!t Men Say to Me: A Poetry Anthology in Response to Toxic Masculinity (2021)
Flower Grand First, Gustavo Hernandez (2021)
Everything is Radiant Between the Hates, Rich Ferguson (2020)
When the Pain Starts: Poetry as Sequential Art, Alan Passman (2020)
This Place Could Be Haunted If I Didn't Believe in Love, Lincoln McElwee (2020)
Impossible Thirst, Kathryn de Lancellotti (2020)
Lullabies for End Times, Jennifer Bradpiece (2020)
Crabgrass World, Robin Axworthy (2020)
Contortionist Tongue, Dania Ayah Alkhouli (2020)
The only thing that makes sense is to grow, Scott Ferry (2020)
Dead Letter Box, Terri Niccum (2019)
Tea and Subtitles: Selected Poems 1999-2019, Michael Miller (2019)
At the Table of the Unknown, Alexandra Umlas (2019)
The Book of Rabbits, Vince Trimboli (2019)
Everything I Write Is a Love Song to the World, David McIntire (2019)
Letters to the Leader, HanaLena Fennel (2019)
Darwin's Garden, Lee Rossi (2019)
Dark Ink: A Poetry Anthology Inspired by Horror (2018)
Drop and Dazzle, Peggy Dobreer (2018)
Junkie Wife, Alexis Rhone Fancher (2018)
The Moon, My Lover, My Mother, & the Dog, Daniel McGinn (2018)
Lullaby of Teeth: An Anthology of Southern California Poetry (2017)
Angels in Seven, Michael Miller (2016)
A Likely Story, Robbi Nester (2014)
Embers on the Stairs, Ruth Bavetta (2014)
The Green of Sunset, John Brantingham (2013)
The Savagery of Bone, Timothy Matthew Perez (2013)
The Silence of Doorways, Sharon Venezio (2013)
Cosmos: An Anthology of Southern California Poetry (2012)
Straws and Shadows, Irena Praitis (2012)

In the Lake of Your Bones, Peggy Dobreer (2012)
I Was Building Up to Something, Susan Davis (2011)
Hopeless Cases, Michael Kramer (2011)
One World, Gail Newman (2011)
What We Ache For, Eric Morago (2010)
Now and Then, Lee Mallory (2009)
Pop Art: An Anthology of Southern California Poetry (2009)
In the Heaven of Never Before, Carine Topal (2008)
A Wild Region, Kate Buckley (2008)
Carving in Bone: An Anthology of Orange County Poetry (2007)
Kindness from a Dark God, Ben Trigg (2007)
A Thin Strand of Lights, Ricki Mandeville (2006)
Sleepyhead Assassins, Mindy Nettifee (2006)
Tide Pools: An Anthology of Orange County Poetry (2006)
Lost American Nights: Lyrics & Poems, Michael Ubaldini (2006)

Patrons

Moon Tide Press would like to thank the following people for their support in helping publish the finest poetry from the Southern California region. To sign up as a patron, visit www.moontidepress. com or send an email to publisher@moontidepress.com.

Anonymous
Robin Axworthy
Conner Brenner
Nicole Connolly
Bill Cushing
Susan Davis
Peggy Dobreer
Dennis Gowans
Alexis Rhone Fancher
Hanalena Fennel
Half Off Books & Brad T. Cox
Donna Hilbert
Jim & Vicky Hoggatt
Michael Kramer
Ron Koertge & Bianca Richards
Gary Jacobelly
Ray & Christi Lacoste
Zachary & Tammy Locklin
Lincoln McElwee
David McIntire
José Enrique Medina
Michael Miller & Rachanee Srisavasdi
Michelle & Robert Miller
Ronny & Richard Morago
Terri Niccum
Andrew November
Jeremy Ra
Luke & Mia Salazar
Jennifer Smith
Andrew Turner
Rex Wilder
Mariano Zaro
Wes Bryan Zwick